For Maura.
Best wishes
Noel.
6/4/2005

Curse of The Birds

Noel Monahan

salmonpoetry

Published in 2000 by
Salmon Publishing Ltd,
Cliffs of Moher, Co. Clare, Ireland
http://www.salmonpoetry.com
email: info@salmonpoetry.com

Copyright © Noel Monahan 2000
The moral right of the author has been asserted.

A catalogue record for this book is available from the British Library.

The Arts Council
An Chomhairle Ealaíon Salmon Publishing gratefully acknowledges the financial assistance of The Arts Council/An Chomhairle Ealaíon.

ISBN 1 897648 95 2 Paperback

All rights reserved. No part of this publication may be reproduced or transmitted in any form or by any means, electronic or mechanical, including photography, recording, or any information storage or retrieval system, without permission in writing from the publisher. The book is sold subject to the condition that it shall not, by way of trade or otherwise, be lent, resold or otherwise circulated without the publisher's prior consent in any form of binding or cover other than that in which it is published and without a similar condition, including this condition, being imposed on the subsequent purchaser.

Cover design by Brenda Dermody
Set by Siobhán Hutson
Printed by Techman Ireland Ltd., Dublin

For Geraldine

Acknowledgements

Acknowledgement is due to the editors of the following in which a number of these poems first appeared:

The Irish Times, The Honest Ulsterman, Books Ireland, Poetry Ireland Review, W.P. Literature and Arts Journal, Argus, The Spark, William Carleton Summer School 1997, The Literary Review (NJ, USA), The Paterson Literary Review (USA), Celtic Visions (Fredericksburg, VA, USA), Or Volge L`Anno: An Anthology of Irish Poets Responding To Leopardi, Tribuna (Romania), Mount Carmel, The Anglo Celt, and *Poets For The Millennium.*

Some of these poems have also been broadcast on RTE Radio 1, Radio Foyle, BBC, Highland Radio (Donegal), and Shannonside/Northern Sound.

Contents

I – Hen People

Hen People	3
The Chair	4
The Corlea Road	5
Carleton's Dream	6
The Dance	8
Waterwords	10
Bungalow	11
The Back Garden	12
Hymn For a Foggy Fair Day	13
The Ghost Shed	16
The New Bypass	18

II – Curse of The Birds

Helen of Troy	23
Bird of Paradise	24
Looking A Bird In the Eye	25
The Swallow's Nest	26
Curse of The Birds	27
The Laughing Field	28
Lough Gowna	29
Sheelin	30
Drumlin Haiku	31
Drumlane	32
Abbeyshrule	33
The Brain Surgeon	34
Sestina	35
The Alhambra	37
The Grand Inquisitor	38
The Skuller	39

III – Mnemosyne Back From Dust

The Haymakers	43
In School	44
The Nuns' Graveyard	45
Donnelly's Bus	46
Dunter	47
Gleann Na nGealt	48
Mnemosyne Back From Dust	49
The Joss-House	50
Lustrations	51
Mobile Confessions	52
Poultry And Politics At The New Museum	53
River Ghost	54
The Predator	55

IV – The Heron and The Stork

Hoof of The Moon	59
The Heron and The Stork	60
A Poem On Your 84th. Birthday	61
Poem For A Lost Brother	62
Brother and Sister	63
It's Wonderful To Be Seven	64
In The Wild Linear Sea	65
Chorus	66
Samhain	67
Christmas Lights	68
The Cave of Ice	69
Hurricane Noel	70
Dawn	71

I

Hen People

Hen People

Dreamy hen-heads nodding
Nipple ochre eyes,
No more wings to beat,
Feathers full of silence.

Heedless and detached,
No more warm eggs
In the nest at home,
No stook left to rest in.

Waxy winter beaks
All around a table,
Heads down for the sip,
Heads up for the slow swallow.

The Chair

Sometimes we say something.
He reaches for his stick,
Walks slowly round and round the chair
Driving off the ghosts that trouble him.

Tired of circling,
He sits back in the chair,
House-flies above his ears,
A frozen bloodshot stare
Waiting for the ghosts to reappear.
Sometimes we say something –
More often,
Nothing.

The Corlea Road

After a long silence
The bog heaved, delivered a road,
So we could see ourselves
In a dark mirror.

I've been sleep-walking
On The Corlea Road,
Listening to iron feet
Trod the night,
Watching young girls stretch their legs
To paint their toe nails.

That grey bearded fellow
With his chin on his knees
Is a story-teller. He believes
The Corlea Road is a highway cover-up
For Midir's mad love for Etain.

Others say the road was never walked,
It's just there between places
For nightmares and dreams.

A road to be abroad on,
In a Ringdong Bog,
Where corduroy lines await music,
Birch lights pole the dark,
Black sleepers stave the clatter of wheels.
Dream road, wooden road,
A road raised up to the light
That will talk,
If you give it time to speak.

Carleton's Dream

Carleton grew tired
Of wakes, cock-fights
And the sesquipedalian words
For the women,
Ardua ad Astra,
Five single notes up his sleeve
He went South.

In Grehan's Inn in Granard,
Ann the goose-girl,
Hopped into his sleep,
Dropped her linsey-woolsey gown
And fled for the fog in the field.

The drills were throbbing,
Thumping and pounding,
A briary bull burst
Through clay and wisps of fog.
William Carleton ran for his life,
The bull pursued him bellowing,
Tail curled, tail erect,
Horn and hoof to ravish him.

William made for the hedge,
Whitethorn, goat willow silvery grey,
Up and over, seven-foot high the lep,
Landed on his feet the far side.
The bull reared on his hind legs,
His long red pencil erect,
Testicles dancing in the sack.

The dream miasma
Puckered Willie's dibble,
Put him off his oats.
He pondered the nightmare,
Willie go easy, he thought to himself,
Taedet me viae.

At Grehan's door in Granard,
He glanced South, turned North,
Back to the home brae,
Mother's milk and flummery.

The Dance

He appeared from nowhere.
Long haired. Dark skinned.
A gleam in his eye.
He was in such demand.

Rows of women,
Especially nurses, sisters,
The entire Nightingale Army,
Swooned before him on the dance floor.

One night a young nurse
From The Surgical,
Felt a huge erection
At a slow dance,

The loverboy rumpled his leather.
She heard a ruckle in his throat,
Saw him squeeze his grapes
And fainted.

Hysteria broke loose.
Cloven feet burst through his suede shoes,
As he vanished through the floorboards
In flames and smoke.

The fathers of the daughters
Were up in arms,
Demanding The Granada Ballroom be closed.
The country bands stopped strumming.
The crowds stopped coming.
The nurses were given night duty.

The story spread everywhere
And the half-lies ran like rain
Across the countryside.
Some said: *He held orgies in the car park.*
Others insisted: *He ran naked through the fields*
Behind the ballroom, with a crowd of women
Round him, shrieking and shaking their hair
And flinging their clothes.

Waterwords

I cross the well stile,
Walk down the grass path.
Ferns uncoil before me, maidenhair
Lounges in the crevices of stone,
Briars hang out roses.
Behind, a Masonic Lodge
Hides in the shadow of trees,
Auld Kirk's eye is on the well.

And I kneel on the mossy water-sill,
Reach my hand in
To comb the surface,
Open the water,
Drawing its darkness
Into white enamel light,
Watching it settle
Into a new shape,
Water falling silverly down the sides.

I play the waterword game,
Shout words at the well's face,
Wait for Auld Kirk to devour them,
Spit them back at me:

Judas	*Ass*
Protestants	*Testants*
Water	*What Are?*
Presbyterians	*Maryannes*
Waterwords	*What Are Words?*

Durken's cattle leave
The scratching-stone to come and listen.
I carry the bucket home
Keeping it clear of seedy grass.

Bungalow

I feel homeless
In the word bungalow
And reach blindly
For a lost stairs,
Hoping to find
The banister of words,
In my fingers,
The ascending lines
Under my feet,
The silence of their song
In my sleep.

The Back Garden
(In response to Giacomo Leopardi's poem, *L'Infinito*.)

The chimney's red bricks
Have come down from the roof
To lie about the garden.

A wellington guffaws
Under a bed in the hedge
At an axle making love
To a wheel.

The jawbone of the mower
Has no teeth left
To bite at the nettles
Behind the ladder.

On an ash-hill, old dandelions
Nod full moon heads at everyone,
The wind whispers across the hedge:
She loves me, she loves me not.

Hymn For A Foggy Fair Day

All the goldenwonder people
Are here,
In from the wild wet townlands
Of the queer names,
Aran-banner noses, cheeks, kerr's-pink,
Bullock-loving, cow-loving men,
A few unbridled widows
In the hoosey drizzle
Of a September Fair morning.

Farmers line the streets,
Fair-sticks raised
Like teeth in the wind,
Carving out spaces for cattle.
Shopkeepers peer shyly
From doors and windows,
Heifers sniff stanchions, cows puck,
Calves hide behind crates,
Ewes, lambs and rams bedraggled
On the bleating lowing streets.

    The Angelus rings.
Hats and caps peel off.
        Behold the creamy smiles
From Miss Tuttle, shop-assistant
As she picks her steps across the street,
Girdle tight conscious.
        Be it done unto the brotherhood
Of the Lamb of God
In the white folds of sleep.

Hail cattle dealers
Pockets full of money,
Hail to a life,
Handling strippers, prodding heifers,
Feeling full udders
And dreaming of cattle ships
Crossing the Irish Sea.
Blessed is Mattie Cadden, white pull-ups,
Hawred boots spattered in dung
As he eyes three two year old heifers
Outside Mixy Sheridan's Drapery.

The sun has come out,
Cattle breath everywhere.
Further down the street
Holy Willie Woods, small son
Of a big cattle dealer stands.
Don't break that man's word, someone shouts,
Now and at the hour
Of dividing tenners, fivers,
Haggling over luck-pennies
But deliver us to the last spit –
The final hand-slap and clench.
Sold ─────────── Amen.

Glory be to all the bare heads
Bent over plates
And to the fair-sticks dropped on the floor
And to the holy steam rising
From wet overcoats,
As you sit around formica-top tables
In the head lowering head lifting motions
At *Tasty Burn's Eaten House*.

Come unto me all ye that labour
And are heavy laden, a Jehovah's Witness says
To a small crowd listening,
On a foggy fair day.

Energies come darkly
Out of blind alleyways,
From Tute's Lane and Porter Row come
Crabby faced men
Beating down the wind,
Blackthorns fat in their hands
As they move through the fair
To fence the preachers in.
Assbraying zealots of the *Dies Irae*,
Making the circle wide,
Mocking the strangers inside, fair-sticks
Drumming, they open a scapegoat path,
Drive them out, down the long line
Past the convent.
Now everything's right as rain, one zealot says
As he returns, checking a knot on his fair-stick.

O Rebus, Dies Irae,
On a foggy fair day,
Hanging by a rainthread
From childhood,
Before the cattle-mart cometh,
Requiescat in pace.

The Ghost Shed

Bold grey blocks, cement outlines,
A roof cruelly red.
Down to earth concerns
Opened on the Westside only
To an orchard of used tyres
Poised on silage,
Black plastic flags flying
In the bushes.

>Ark of concrete
>Silage cafe
>Slither of cowdung
>Slurry pit full.

Sleeveen watches his beasts
In the night lights
Of his newly-built shed,
Knows them by their rump numbers,
Listens to the black and white rhythm
Of their ruminations,
On the close-circuit TV
At the foot of his bed.

>Ark of concrete
>Silage cafe
>Slither of cowdung
>Slurry pit full.

Moonfarmers wander in
From lost cow-tracks, buckets over their heads.
They gape furiously

Through rusty holes,
Ghosting and talking to themselves
About strawy days, a ramshackle shed,
The white cow who gave milk
Till she bled.

   Fading moonbeam
   Morning blue and green,
   Meadow-sweet, cowslip by the lake
   Song of the corncrake.

Ark of concrete	Fading moonbeam
Silage cafe	Morning blue and green
Slither of cowdung	Meadow-sweet, cowslip by the lake
Slurry pit full	Song of the corncrake

  Black mitred fowl, talons tight
  On a satellite dish, crowcaw-caw-caw...
  Threaten the ancestral ghosts.
  The lost souls
  Unbucket their heads,
  Give one long last ghostly bucket-concerto
  And leave
  For the fields of the moon.

The New Bypass

There went out a decree from the County Manager:
All crossroads come to roundabouts,
Now and in the last hours of the millennium.
And behold the bypass came to pass.

I am the way,
The blood and the tar.
I will open millions of cat's-eyes
In the dark.

And there were roadworks everywhere.
A flotilla of red and white buntings across barrels,
Manholes popping up, country streams forced underground.
The yellow Akerman scooped the crossroads in his
    pincer-jaws
And laid it on a trailer.

I am the way
The blood and the tar.
I will open millions of cat's-eyes
In the dark.

Komatsu, Kobelco, Hitachi
Caterpillared drumlins to clay and water.
An amber procession of clay moved past
Pentecostal stones shouting in red lorries:
Navel stones, altar stones, cursing stones,
Stones of destiny, stones upon stones
Systoling and diastoling away from the heart
Of the provincial town.

I am the way
The blood and the tar.
I will open millions of cat's-eyes
In the dark.

The lamb is a lost soul by the roadside.
The shepherd was killed at a Black Spot.
Umpteen advertisements in huge letters:
ESSO, TEXACO, COCA COLA
Line the highway.

I am the way
The blood and the tar.
I will open millions of cat's-eyes
In the dark.

Speed limits flash across radio chat shows,
CD music whizzes past the whispers
Of lost fields, forgotten towns, dancing at the crossroads.
O Christ, turn up the volume,
Keep the rhythm coming on the goddamn road.

I am the way
The blood and the tar.
I will open millions of cat's-eyes
In the dark.

II

Curse of The Birds

Helen Of Troy

A laughing yolk,
Crying white,
Tapped on the shell
And a bird came out
To sing.

Bird Of Paradise

When the bird flew through
The roof window,
The young woman was flustered.

He wrapped his wings
round her, dropped his feathers
To tread her where she stood.

He whispered some taboo
About the fledgling son to come,
Said it was forbidden him to hunt for birds.

Then he limpwinged back
To his holy tree
Leaving her cob-swanned and airy.

Looking A Bird In The Eye

I'm watching a thrush
Come and go
With a shawl of moss
On her head.

And the thrush takes my ribs,
To carry them as twigs
To her nest, the inside she lines
With the hair on my head.

My head is a bird's nest
Sitting in the box-wood,
My eyes, blue eggs.

And in every April wind
Blue eggs dance.

The Swallow's Nest

Almost April,
Each mud-eye
Is a word of mouth
Calling them back
To patch the wall
In the halfway house.

Curse Of The Birds

The boy who robbed the nest,
Ate the swallow's eggs,
Is plucking

Devil's-bit by night
Down in the wetlands
On his knees,

Beak to the ground,
Curls stretching into feathers,
The moon is hatching in his head.

The Laughing Field

The man couldn't sleep
With all the laughing.
He blamed it on the stones
And drowned them in the river.

The laughing continued.
He blamed the thistles,
And burnt them in the ditches.

Still the laughing:
People told him it was the fairy thimbles,
Others said it was the crows
Laughing their beaks off in the dark.

He left the bed,
Ran blindly round the field,
Looking for crows till he fell:
Tiuc, Tiuc, Tiuc, he cried from his hunkers
And he never got up with the laughing.

Lough Gowna

A woman washing
Saw his eyes
Through the sweet water
In the well at Rathbracken,
His hooves pulling free
Of the earth,
His calf head breaking the water.

She stroked his long wet back
With dry grass,
Legs slowly stretching,
His mouth reaching for the first milk.

Only close awhile,
The calf broke clear
Of the well and the woman,
Burst past the bush in the gap,
Down through the fields and meadows,
A long river trailing his tail.

The hills shaped a lake
In the valley,
Reeds grew, trout hatched,
 Swans came to nest
And through the lake's big eye
The calf looks up at the sky.

Sheelin

One rainy summer
I fell into Sheelin.
She took me to a sunken road

That led to drowned fields,
Full of grazing brown trout,
Bare limbed women

Saving hay
On the white swarths of water.
Lovely Inny slipping down the backwash.

Drumlin Haiku

Rosary of hills
Chained to the cold religion
Of the ice goddess.

Drumlane

I met a madman
In the graveyard

Singing to a crow that was perched
On an abbot's stone head.

The crow grew tired
Of the insane psalm,

Plunged into a nearby lake
And the madman turned to sing to me.

Abbeyshrule

They were all peering
At me in Abbeyshrule,
Little tonsured men
Down at the bridge, up the trees,
Behind headstones, gates and gables.

And they inveigled me
Down to the ruins
Of the abbey by the stream,
Leaving the everyday words for Latin.

When I sang
Stabat Mater Dolorosa
Before an altar of nettles,
Blackbirds and starlings
Flew from the vestry.

Back in the local
I drank Guinness,
'Told them the village was alive
With the ghosts of dead monks.

The Brain Surgeon

Bricin the Brain Surgeon
Drilled a hole in Cenn Faelad's head,
After the poor man's skull
Was bashed in war.

Bricin put a hand
Into the branches of the brain
And made rearrangements,
Leaving him with the one defect
Of not being able to forget.

Cenn Faelad took to the learning,
Wrote volumes on vellum,
Praising saints and scholars
And Bricin the Brain Surgeon.

Sestina

For Simion and Hannah

Manole, the master builder had a dream.
He looked at the sky,
Saw a line of coloured stones
Ascending to the highest tower,
Birds with broad wings
Beating down the rain, making tears.

When his wife got in the way of the dream,
He placed a ring of stones
About her thighs, walled her in a tower,
Leaving her without the blue of the sky,
No bird on wings,
Only the darkness and her tears.

The King grew jealous of Manole's tower,
Removed all the ladders from the sky,
Leaving the master-builder in tears,
To stare into the walls of his dream,
Fill the mouth of morning with atoms of stone
And no way down except on wings.

Locked into his tower,
Clinging to one final dream,
Manole took the raw stones,
Dressed them into feathers to make wings.
The hard facts of stone drew tears
From an inner wound that drove him to the sky.

The night before he spread his wings,
Manole sat still in the tower,

Contemplating the desert of stones,
The tower that baited him to the sky,
The emptiness of a dream
That lead him to bury his wife's tears.

The wind ambushed his dream.
Manole fell through a hole in the sky.
Down and down to the judder of his wings,
Striking belfries, knocking clock-hands off towers,
Crashing into the street with wings of stone,
The crowd gathered round, reduced to tears.

Manole, your dream survives your broken wings.
The stones of Curtea de Arges stand in a Romanian sky
Testimony to your tears, Master Builder of the tower.

The Alhambra

Is a sky and water landscape
Where Koran and Bible meet,
A floating history

On a mirror of water
With only the sun
To turn back the pages.

Honeycomb of flowers and stars,
Twelve lions with the shock
Of earthquake on their faces

Stare into a Heaven on earth,
A palace of Kings, home to beggars,
Refuge for dreams and stories

Of ghosts running into walls,
Aerial fishermen hooking swallows
With flies from the sky.

Where sun and snow
Pour light and water
On the *Hill of Tears*

And the sigh of the Moor
Is heard in the myrtle hedges
Begging for silence.

The Grand Inquisitor

The Grand Inquisitor
Of Granard
Sat on our heads
And hatched The Elephant
Of The Unforgettable.

The Skuller

The heifer is dragged out.
Chains pulled through a noose
She slithers on gravel,
One late burst and bellow,
As they lace her legs together.

The skuller sits on the forelegs,
Slips a jute bag under her head.
She lies there, teeth gritting,
Big nostrils running.

He snips at the hairy flesh
With a breadknife,
Angles the saw
For the deep cut.

Blood rains down
On the stones,
The stumps he washes
With a rag from a bucket,
Coats them in bronze
With iodine strokes from a feather.

III

Mnemosyne Back From Dust

The Haymakers

In the blur of nightfall,
The meadow is full of white torsos,
Happily tossing grass
At the moon.

In School

We remembered and forgot,
We repeated, remembered and forgot,
We recited and forgot.
We chalked on slates,
We rubbed it out.
We did sums with pencils.
We dipped into inkwells,
We made letters with pen and ink,
    small letters between blue lines
    BIG LETTERS BETWEEN RED LINES.
We crossed out words,
We crossed out lines.
We soaked up blobs
    on pink blotting paper.

The school added us.
The school subtracted us.
The school multiplied us.
The school divided us.

The Nuns' Graveyard

Old nuns live here
All travellers once
On the road.

Chalk in their hands,
Talking in their sleep
To a classroom of girls in blue dresses.

A family of women,
Drawn to the words of the Father,
Cutting chrysanthemums,
Leafing through missals,
Siren sisters in the choir.

Old brides, all married once
To the same man,
Clinging to his hem, drinking his wine.

Old nuns live here
All travellers once
Waiting for lightening to strike.

Donnelly's Bus

On Donnelly's Bus
All the dead passengers sit up.
I hear skeleton conversations
Rattling down the aisle,
Archie, the ghost driver
Overfeeding the throttle.

On Donnelly's Bus
Phantom passengers lean on gravestones.
The man with the pipe is an Indian Chief
Lost to a language of smoke.
Gent Geraghty's white scarf is wrapped
Tight as a bandage round his throat.

On Donnelly's Bus
Dream faces peer
Through beads of rain
At waltzing fields and ditches.
Elmbank Chickens in cardboard boxes
Peck at the light in my head.

Dunter

Dunter Donohoe tip taps on the last,
A necklace of sprigs on his lips,
Hand to mouth motions,
He clusters soles and heels
With silver stars,
Spits kisses
To butter the leather.

Silent shoe tongues
Cower in the corner,
Old wrinkled soles lie dusty dead,
White baby-boots walk in their sleep,
Dunter hears the squelch
Of leaking boots coming down the hill
And smiles forever.

His pale wife sits by the window,
Waiting for the evening star:
> *She who shows the way*
> *To the other stars*
> *And brings us dreams.*

Gleann Na nGealt

For Tom MacIntyre

Quiet as a pike
At the bottom of a winter lake,
Pulling brosna
From ditches at dusk,
Watchful of the stars, given to dreams,
Eating sorrel in yesterday's meadow.
Straying across fields, hermit
In a wilderness of windmills,
With a small bird perched
On his big toe, a poem
On the tip of his tongue.

Mnemosyne Back From Dust
(centenary celebration poem to Austin Clarke, 1996.)

When Austin Clarke began to hum,
The ruling bees were honeymooning
In a new cosy hive,
Gorging themselves,
Taking little notice of his craft
And when he stung,
Or so they said he did,
They drove him off.

Free from the other bees
He found his own hedge-hive
At the far edge of chanting hours,
Sang *suantraí*, humming home
From fields of flowers,
Hymen hymns that rocked
The pollen-sacs on pulpits,
Shook the stamens of the little shops
Through their petal doors and windows.

The Joss-House
(In response to Louis MacNeice's *Autumn Journal*, section 3.
Most are accepters, born and bred to harness.)

There's a vacancy
For the post of god
Of walls and ditches
In the joss-house.

To get past the door gods,
Applicants should be familiar
With the josser's smile,
Have a primary degree in Confucianism,
And a willingness
To answer the gong.

Lustrations

Have a lorry load
Of priests in here
Immediately,
Fifteen, at least,
To hear confessions.
Bring Ajax, Daz,
Surf and other detergents
For the *remissionem peccatorum*.

And make them conjugate
The verb to sin
In every mood and tense,
Steaming suds rising
To drown their dreams,
Gauzy souls hanging from the blackboards,
Slowly drip-drying
In the asylum of chalk and talk.

Mobile Confessions

Father Quasimodo of the mobile phone
Lost to the trickery
Of his plastic machine,
Bends to erect his aerial
Like some grand seigneur
In the seraglio
And with a wave of a hand
He gives absolutely
Super fast absolutions
To his lady Madonnas.

Poultry And Politics At The New Museum

When Councillor C. Rooster
Cock-a-doodled
Before the break of days,
The chamber capons came together
For cocktails and truffle.

They roosted momentarily,
In a half-ready shrine
To their glorious past,
Wings tensed, eyes half shut,
Red coxcombs combing
The unholy itch of
You scratch my back
I'll scratch yours:
Cockernony cockalorum
In saecula saeculorum.

River Ghost

When a priest drove him out
From the house,
He was trapped
Between the froth and the water.

At the bridge,
We dropped stones,
Felt the chill of his eye
Looking up.

The Predator

Is ring-master of the prayer-wheel.
Laughing in the centre, whip in hand,
Black leaf hat, featherblack soutane,
A long leather beak stuffed
With smarties, mars-bars, rolos ...

He glances at the children
Out of the corners of his egg-shell eyes,
Removes his beak to disarm them
As they circle and fall:

> *Ring-a-ring o' roses,*
> *A pocket full of posies,*
> *Atishoo – Atishoo –*
> *We all fall down.*

IV

The Heron and The Stork

Hoof Of The Moon

I see your horse eyes
In the night.

Hear a blacksmith's anvil sing
Through chains of rain.

Night's sickle hoof
Kicks at the traces of sleep.

The hollow house is breathing slowly,
A horseman is waiting.

The Heron And The Stork

When the heron flies out
Her broad wings roof the river
In grey feathers.

The stork, who fed the heron
In old age,
Floods the river with light,

Lifting the grey.
The stork and the heron
Are birds of the one feather.

A Poem On Your 84th. Birthday

I hunger for the few unburied words
Left you
In the fields
Of the red marsh.

I feed you place names,
Curraghroe, you consume
Like a first communion
And from your gutted field
You raise a birdsong
That sings of heaven.

Poem For A Lost Brother

Old dried thistle heads
Stake the heart of winter,
Hare and fox tracks
Line the white field,
Unexpected twists and turns
Shimmer like constellations,
Slowing down the long silent lines
Of unspoken words
That trace your baby fingers
Along the forehead of the hill.

Brother And Sister
for Geraldine

It could be a mourning or a celebration.
Here they stand in black and white,
Two snap-shot figures,
Pretending to shy away from the attention
Of having their photo taken.

He's himself,
A boy butler in bow-tie,
Double-breasted suit,
With an eager to please smile.

She's resigned
To the flowery dress, the big white ribbon
On her head. And she knows
He needs her company
On this First Communion Day.

It's Wonderful To Be Seven
(For Ciara on her seventh birthday)

Sing seven starry notes
For seven candles burning,
Seven apples shining
On the plough.

Sing seven happy notes
For seven petals unfolding,
Seven colours glowing
Through the rain.

In The Wild Linear Sea

for Niall, Cian and Ronan

Their limbs are lines of force
Galloping across wet sand
In the wild linear sea.

Three brothers smashing fear,
Horse-kicking glass waves,
Their limbs are lines of force.

Their brilliant sea-clothing
Hanging on a clothes-line
In the wild linear sea.

Water-stallions lusting
For the swirl and the swish,
Their limbs are lines of force.

They curse with no remorse
Above the thundering waves
In the wild linear sea.

Hoof-trotting back to me,
Nut-brown in sand and sea,
Their limbs are lines of force
In the wild linear sea.

Chorus

Our voices call out
From the sand-towns
Of lost dreams, tumbling castles
That may be swept away
By tomorrow.

And in an unyielding tide
Of breath,
We build and rebuild
Our lives
In a sea of sand.

Samhain

She is the white breath,
Passing through a chink in the wall.
Courted from either side
By a line of kisses,
She breathes her first November song.

Christmas Lights

When my father brought me
To the Dagger's Hill
To see the Christmas lights,
How small the townlands seemed,
Candle flame in every window
Was Holy ... Holy ... Holy ...
In the little rootlands,
Where every flicker was a poem
Setting my heart on fire,
Touching my soul
Before the world grew old.

The Cave Of Ice

The donkey's creels are full of snow
To carry winter to the manger.

The green tree comes inside,
Fish swim on the walls.

A mother in bindweed
Sings by the cradle:

Altar of nails,
Crib and crypt,
Ghosts dance
Around the word
And seeds sleep
In winter peace.

Hurricane Noel

It was a red wind,
Stones ran together
Like mice across the road,
Trees carolled, dogs howled
At bandanas in the bushes.

Branches walloped the windscreen,
The baby flung from the stable
Came crashing through blades of rain,
A Christmas Tree fell across the road,
One gate locked into another
Came tumbling through the fields.

The power lines fell,
Wise men no longer wise,
Groped in the dark
For gas, generators and candles,
Red sparks of holly fired the moon.

Dawn

Out here ... morning is everywhere,
It feels so long ago,
The hills come down
From the rafters of ice
The lakes come up through the floor
Living together like man and wife.